Rakan Brahedni is a technologist, futurist, certified health coach, and father-of-two on a mission to inspire others to live more mindful and meaningful lives with the hope of building a better world for future generations. He and his family reside in Dubai where he is currently working on his second book.

To my daughters.

Rakan Brahedni

MINDFUL FUTURISM: PAVING THE WAY FOR FUTURE GENERATIONS

AUSTIN MACAULEY PUBLISHERS™
LONDON • CAMBRIDGE • NEW YORK • SHARJAH

Copyright © Rakan Brahedni 2024

The right of Rakan Brahedni to be identified as author of this work has been asserted by the author in accordance with Federal Law No. (7) of UAE, Year 2002, Concerning Copyrights and Neighboring Rights.

All rights reserved. No part of this publication may be reproduced, stored in a retrieval system, or transmitted in any form or by any means, electronic, mechanical, photocopying, recording, or otherwise, without the prior permission of the publishers.

Any person who commits any unauthorized act in relation to this publication may be liable to legal prosecution and civil claims for damages.

The age group that matches the content of the books has been classified according to the age classification system issued by the Ministry of Culture and Youth.

ISBN – 9789948778004 – (Paperback)
ISBN – 9789948778011 – (E-Book)

Application Number: MC-10-01-8204661
Age Classification: E

Printer Name: iPrint Global Ltd
Printer Address: Witchford, England

First Published 2024
AUSTIN MACAULEY PUBLISHERS FZE
Sharjah Publishing City
P.O Box [519201]
Sharjah, UAE
www.austinmacauley.ae
+971 655 95 202

Table of Contents

1. Genesis	**9**
2. The Era of Mindlessness	**17**
3. State of the World	**29**
From God-Made to Man-Made Food	*31*
From Healthcare to Sick Care	*34*
From Progression to Regression	*36*
The End of an Era	*39*
4. The River We Live Upon	**41**
5. Ending the Era of Mindlessness	**47**
The Three Principles	*54*
The First Principle: Accept Responsibility	55
The Second Principle: Acknowledge Impact	56
The Third Principle: Act Deliberately	57
The Three Steps	*58*
Step 1: Identifying Purpose	59
Step 2: Apply Due Diligence	59
Step 3: Make Your Decision	60

6. The Trodden Path 61

Case Study: "Free at Last" 64

7. The Next Step 80

1. Genesis

She looked helpless. This tiny, brand-new human being had just entered the world, and she was my responsibility. This thought hit me like a truck, and I ran out of the hospital in a total panic.

Outside, I desperately tried to come to terms with what was happening. I'd spent the last nine months preparing myself for fatherhood and the permanency of my role to come, but nothing could have prepared me for the wave of emotions that crashed over me the moment I gazed upon my beautiful daughter for the very first time. I was instantly in love, yet overwhelmed with feelings of responsibility, self-doubt, and fear of failure.

I paced back and forth on the sidewalk, sifting through everything that was racing through my mind. *The world is a total mess*, I thought, realizing the odds were seemingly stacked against me as a parent. I had so much to learn, and even more to battle against, if I was going to provide my daughter with the upbringing she deserved.

At that moment, I had a profound realization: there were only two options. The first was to panic. And although my anxiety was kicking in greater than ever, the idea of raising my daughter in a state of fear just wasn't an option. The second one seemed to be the only sensible choice to me—to fight against those odds and work toward creating a better future for her.

Clarity, finally. My body calmed down, my mind settled, and I knew with complete certainty what I had to do. I was more fearful than ever but felt my courage rising to the surface. My daughter needed me to be strong, and this duty was both motivating and comforting. I regained my composure and returned to the ward.

It wasn't until much later that day that I was able to hold her for the first time. I was dreading it as much as I was longing for it. But as the nurse placed her in my arms, her tiny body resting upon me ever so trustingly, I felt a profound sense of responsibility. I was going to have to feed her, clothe her, comfort her, educate her, protect her, and so much more. But I felt a much greater sense of duty than merely providing for her basic needs. I was going to have to make the world a better place for her, and I had no idea what this would look like or entail. Still, clearer than anything ever before, I realized that this was going to be my mission in life.

In the following days, as I began to learn the ropes of parenting, my newfound purpose began to take firm hold of me. It sliced through my anxiety and brought solace in my most fearful moments.

A few days after we returned home from the hospital, I was assigned my first parenting task: buy a baby bottle for storing breast milk in the fridge. Simple enough. I went to the store, grabbed a bottle off the shelf, and headed to pay. "Is this a good brand?" I wondered, as I handed the bottle to the cashier. I whipped out my phone and did a quick search.

Mixed reviews created some doubt in my mind, so I headed back to review my options. Standing in the middle of the aisle, facing a sea of packaging, I was suddenly overwhelmed by the plethora of brands and models to choose from. Some were plastic, others glass, some made in Germany, others in China. I weighed up the options, grabbed what appeared to be the best one, and returned home to do more research.

I learned about the various brands, and the variety of bottle shapes, attachments, and accessories that each had to offer. The most interesting—and alarming—part of my research was when I began to read up about the materials baby bottles were made from.

I read about the benefits of glass versus plastic, the dangers of BPA and other chemicals that were proven to be incredibly harmful to a child's cognitive and physical development, and how microwaving plastic bottles caused these chemicals to leach into breast milk.

This went on and on. I went from one topic to the next, and within a few weeks I became an expert in baby bottles. We now had a variety of the best and safest bottles, science-backed procedures for cleaning them and, most importantly, peace of mind in knowing that we did our best.

My research consumed many hours, but knowing that I saved my daughter from numerous harmful chemicals and other dangers made it worth my while. Researching the heck out of everything became my thing. Whenever we had to buy something for her, I would arm myself with science and reviews from other parents. Whenever I entered a baby shop or pharmacy, I knew exactly what to look for and what to avoid.

I was a minesweeper in a vast and dangerous ocean of questionable baby products.

After several months of studying every purchasing decision I made for my daughter, a profound realization dawned upon me: why did I have to be doing all this investigating? Why were there so many risks to be wary of in the first place? Something was clearly wrong.

These thoughts haunted me for weeks to come. Confronting how little I knew about baby products had opened my eyes to the fact that I knew very little about the rest of my purchasing decisions. I opened the Pandora's Box and my life changed forever. In the following months, I tumbled deeper down the rabbit hole. I studied the effects of plastics and chemicals on our hormones and other biological functions. I learned about the vast amount of toxins and pollutants in the air we breathe, the soaps and shampoos we use, and the food we eat. It was enlightening, but quite frightening.

Despite living in an era of incredible intelligence, technological marvels and countless scientific breakthroughs, why do we have to be so cautiously vigilant in the simplest daily choices just to avoid unnecessary harm? How is our system so broken, yet so acceptable to the vast majority of people, including myself?

Some of this information wasn't really news to me, but I had accepted it as a fact of life. As many of us do, I would eat junk food knowing it was rife with harmful fats, additives, and preservatives. I knew it was unhealthy but the risk seemed acceptable.

As the evidence mounted, I felt fooled and foolish. I had spent years completely oblivious to the sheer volume of dangers I was exposed to every single day. My feelings of shame quickly turned into anger. Prompted by this life-altering realization, and my recently discovered mission in life, I quit my job.

I had spent years playing it safe, not venturing out into the world and felt I had limited my professional opportunities in doing so. To disrupt the stagnation, my wife, daughter and I packed up our lives and spent the next three years traveling the world. I set my intention on finding a role that would allow me to make a real impact. I had no clue where I would end up, but I was excited and fueled by the adventure of it all. Our travels led us to the United Kingdom, and eventually Denmark, where I found the opportunity to work at the headquarters of LEGO, an organization that later shifted my view of what the corporate world was capable of.

I was ecstatic to land such an opportunity and contribute to a mission that impacted my own childhood. LEGO had spent decades inspiring and educating children, but I had no clue how much brain power and sheer love was behind every product they manufactured. Working for LEGO allowed me to experience this process firsthand, and it changed me forever. I learned the significance of truly loving my customers and consumers. In doing so, every facet of my work became a labor of love, underscored with caution and care.

One lesson in particular impacted me greater than any other I'd had before or since: it's not about "doing no harm." It's about "doing as much good as possible." This was present in the speech and work of every one of my colleagues.

Everyone, from the janitors to the CEO, was committed to delivering the best possible work that they could. And in the spirit of the company's founding culture, only the best was good enough.

Circumstances soon brought me back to Dubai, my family's home for many years, and although I had been on an incredible journey, I eventually began to lose hope in my dreams of changing the world. Despite my best efforts, I found myself back where I started—feeling disconnected and lost. I felt I had been naïve, overzealous, and unrealistic in trying to take on such a monstrous task. Feeling defeated, I gave up, but found comfort in just focusing on what I could do for my daughter.

Dubai is renowned for its culture of risk-taking and daring innovation, and as fate would have it, I soon landed a role that would, for the first time in my professional career, give me an opportunity to potentially create impact on a global scale. Working in innovation, I was encouraged to dream big and envision a better world. It was fulfilling and inspiring and stirred up my old desires to make a difference.

Through my work I had access to some incredible people: lawmakers, government officials, high-powered executives, billionaires, academics, scientists, economists—real change-makers. I was fortunate enough to meet, work, and learn from a number of these people. There was one conversation in particular that changed everything for me.

I had a mentor whom I respected a great deal. He was smart, inspiring and quite influential. While driving to work one day, I saw a large advertisement for a new fast-food meal.

It was overwhelmingly in-your-face and was clearly targeting children. But then I saw another one, and another, and another—brand after brand promoting disgusting, unhealthy food. I thought about how these ads could affect my daughter and other children. They were meant to influence, and certainly would. Frustrated by them, I approached my mentor and asked what could be done to ban these companies from such blatant and dangerous methods to drive their sales. "Banning these companies from advertising isn't the solution," he said. "If you want things to change, then educate people. Real change happens when people do."

At this moment, the biggest, brightest light bulb lit up inside my head. My dreams of changing the world, and the seemingly impossible task of changing the way brands and manufacturers operated suddenly seemed possible—but it would have to come from the people.

My daughter was now five years old and for the first time, the pieces were finally falling into place. My mission no longer seemed naive, or impossible. I wasn't replacing a dream of changing the way brands and manufacturers operated with an even bigger dream of changing the minds of every person on earth—I was simply going to devise a plan, share it with the world, and that would be my contribution. I accepted that I may never change the world, but what I had learned through my journey was valuable enough to share, and if I could change the thinking pattern of a single person, I would have succeeded.

I was energized, reinvigorated, and ready to make things happen.

Throughout my career, I was taught to think far into the future, envision a better world, and strategically design solutions that were feasible, impactful, and realistic. I had exactly what I needed to accomplish my mission. I used these tools to extrapolate what I had learned and applied with my daughter and created a method that everyone could use.

For the next year, I worked on devising a simple system with logical steps that could be applied to virtually any decision in life, whether it was as small as deciding on which baby bottle to buy, or something as critical as manufacturing a new medicine. It's meant to be grounded in common sense, tapping into human beings' innate desires to do good and be good. I've called it "Mindful Futurism." In its application, perhaps we can build a better future for ourselves and the generations to come.

Mindful Futurism is the antidote to a broken mindset which lies at the root of our biggest global problems—pollution, soil erosion, climate change, warfare, and poverty. It's a deeply entrenched paradigm with thousands of years of momentum. And modern civilization is founded on it.

2. The Era of Mindlessness

The human body and mind are truly awesome. We're born totally dependent and unable to comprehend much. But within a few short years we're able to perform complex tasks like walking, talking and solving puzzles, demonstrating signs of incredible intelligence.

Our bodies are made up of water and tissue, yet can withstand extreme physical exertion and even abuse over entire lifetimes. We are built to survive and can take quite the beating—physically, mentally, and emotionally.

Despite our strength and resilience, we're also incredibly fragile. As COVID-19 ravaged our way of life in 2020 and the years to follow, like many other pandemics before, we were given a stark reminder of how something invisible to the naked eye is all it takes to wreak havoc and destroy the lives of millions.

And our minds, as incredible and beautiful as they may be, can be distorted, disrupted, and even destroyed through a single metaphysical experience. A small dose of a psychoactive substance is all it takes to damage mental function, erase memories or create powerful psychological experiences.

Far too often we forget our fragility. We forget that we're born helpless and dependent on the help of others. Without the help of doctors, midwives, and nurses, our entry into the world would be a struggle for us and our parents. Without our mothers' bosoms, we would lack the sustenance and human connection we need to thrive. Without our teachers and tutors, we would struggle to learn, or learn very little. Without our governments and the support of civil servants, we would lack the infrastructure and security essential to the development of society. We're born needing others to survive and thrive, but as soon as we establish any kind of independence, or can generate an income for ourselves, we seem to forget this reliance, and credit ourselves with having "made it on our own."

From the moment we're born until our death, living is almost all about surviving. Whether it's the basics of eating and drinking, or our more modern and complex needs for technology, connectivity, and transport, we're constantly on the hunt for resources, fighting for survival in one way or another.

If we went back in time, surviving would have probably involved fending off wild animals or other physical threats. It would have entailed taking precautions and actions to stay alive. Fast forward to today and our definition has changed quite drastically. Rather than immediate threats, the concept of staying alive is now about fighting off slow killers, quite a fitting description in this day and age, where our biggest killers quite literally take decades, or even entire lifetimes, to lay us to rest.

Yet despite the relative lack of predators, invaders, or concern for starvation, we still operate as if we're under immediate threat. Our bodies are regularly flooded with adrenaline and cortisol. Our sympathetic nervous systems are on full alert, as if we were standing just feet away from the edge of a cliff or within swiping range of a tiger's deadly claws.

It's clear that our instinctual responses are misplaced. We're constantly fighting for survival but our greatest threats are, for the most part, self-inflicted or at the very least avoidable. Our diets are horribly unbalanced. Our food is filled with chemicals, pesticides, hormones, and antibiotics, all of which have been proven to contribute to or even cause common fatal diseases. We're surrounded by pollutants, toxins, and other environmental contaminants, slowly edging us toward illness. Our lifestyles are fast-paced, stress-filled, and the biggest drivers of early death.

We spend virtually every single day of our lives in maintenance mode. We must sleep, eat, drink, bathe and clothe ourselves, brush our teeth, exercise and so much more. We study to earn degrees to acquire jobs to earn money to pay for the things we need to maintain ourselves. No job means no home. No home means no security, no bed, no kitchen, no bathroom. The most critical essentials to our survival now come at a price.

Once upon a time, our ancestors would simply venture out into the wilderness for a suitable piece of land to build a house and then forage for food and clean water each day. Today, we must "earn a living." Have you ever thought about that phrase?

At some point, we decided that living had to be earned, despite the fact that it is an unquestionable human right. None of us chose to be here, but we all have to live. "Living" should not have to be earned.

Modern life, however, certainly does. The luxuries of technology and the modernity of our lifestyles certainly come at a price. But as humans born to this earth with equal rights, we should be free to live at no cost beyond that of our own efforts.

The industrial revolution could probably be credited with being the biggest driving force toward this now acceptable way of life. People have been buying and selling things for thousands of years. There have always been rich and poor people. There have always been luxuries that are unaffordable to the masses. The imbalance of wealth that we see today isn't as new as some people may think.

But throughout history, mankind had the freedom to build their own homes and forage for resources. Over time, ownership began being declared over lands and territories by the rich and powerful, and the masses became more and more restricted as to what they could freely claim as their own. The industrial revolution added fuel to this fire, allowing people to manufacture and sell goods like never before. This meant more wealth, and faster, bringing with it more power and influence over the world.

Within each of us is a mechanism that creates an intrinsic desire to survive and thrive. This mechanism is the ego. When in check, it allows us to have a sense of self-worth. It allows us to believe that we deserve to live, that we deserve better.

It helps keep us moving in an upward trajectory, always trying to better our circumstances and ensure we have the resources needed to flourish. But when the ego is allowed to grow beyond a healthy limit, it breeds greed. Combined with our basic instinct to survive, greed becomes justified within our minds. This isn't an attack on rich industrialists or the global "elite"—we are all guilty of this greed to some extent. We're no longer merely trying to survive. We're now trying to thrive.

As businesses began to expand their wealth in the late nineteenth century and into the twentieth, their influence and power grew. They went from selling hundreds of items a day to hundreds of millions. New technologies allowed them to manufacture products never seen before: ingenious devices to make people's lives easier, and disposable products that brought about incredible convenience. All of this new "stuff" created excitement, and with this excitement came urgency. Businesses have always competed, but now there was more at stake. New transportation methods and infrastructure allowed for greater distribution networks and wider reach. This meant more customers, and therefore more money, influence, and power up for grabs.

With businesses competing so fiercely, customers began to have more options. People could now choose from a plethora of makes, models, and variants, effectively shifting power into the hands of the consumer. But it wasn't long before businesses began to fight back, rapidly renovating and innovating to regain control over their markets.

The best and the brightest were recruited to capture new audiences through powerful and creative messaging and to keep existing consumers hooked by engineering new reasons for them to continue buying existing products.

Some incredible organizations came to life. They influenced cultures and shaped economies. They changed what we eat and drink, how we dress, our daily routines and pastimes, and so much more. Fast forward to today, and the world is influenced and in many ways ruled by companies hoarding wealth greater than entire countries.

The fierceness of this competition and the urgency behind being the first, best and biggest, drove these organizations to invent. This dawned an era of technological advancements unlike any other time in documented history. Advances in transportation, telecommunication, healthcare, education, and pretty much everything in between, have created the world that we live in today. For the most part, we are safer, more connected, better educated and live longer than the generations before us.

Alas, the time to take heed is upon us. We have raced through the twentieth century and into the first decades of the twenty-first, releasing product after product, innovation after innovation. Fueled by our instinctive need to survive, our egos have taken over, and we are in an endless pursuit of money and power. We've gone from creating businesses to creating entire industries and markets. Business is so deeply ingrained in our humanity that our educational system—from the earliest years all the way through to adulthood—is designed to shape us and prepare us to get a job within an existing business or begin one ourselves.

In a matter of a hundred years or so, we went from being a species capable of surviving in the wild—able to find fresh water and forage for food—to one that wouldn't survive without being catered to by businesses. We no longer know how to forage or hunt. One may argue that foraging and hunting have been replaced with working and "earning a living," but that is a dangerous notion. It is one that ties our survival to the commercial interests of others. It's also vastly more complex than our dependence on the planet's natural resources.

Instead of simply venturing out into the world, taking with us a few tools and knowledge passed down from the generations before us, we now have to embark on a lifetime of learning and hard work to afford the essentials of life. We were once able to build a home on a vacant plot of land. Now, we're tied to rental agreements, mortgages, and loans. We own so much in terms of material possessions, but most of us can't even afford our own homes.

We've created a complex and highly interconnected world, and time is of the essence. Everything we do is tied to time, and there never seems to be enough of it. We need to be first to market, first to the office, first in line. We need to rush to the office, rush to the meeting, rush back home.

The slow burn of our education through school and university seems to never end. The second we graduate, the pistol fires and the race is on. We land our first jobs, excited to venture out into the world. By then, we've spent years waiting for our freedom, and with it the opportunity to prove ourselves worthy to the generations before us.

Our first jobs bring our first paychecks, first apartments, and first cars. It's exciting and rewarding. For the fortunate among us, we are finally unleashed toward abundance. We're no longer restricted by the constraints set by our parents or circumstances. Need more money? Save, ask for a promotion, put in a few extra shifts, get a second job, find a new job, take out a loan. The options are as abundant as the "stuff" we have access to and want.

We race through our twenties and thirties, some of us getting married and having children along the way. Before we know it, we're preparing to pass the baton onto the next generation to continue the race.

By the time we're in our forties and fifties, our priorities begin to shift toward family, friends, and health. Many of us are left unfulfilled by decades of obsessive racing, and seek greater meaning to life. Before we know it, our kids begin venturing out into the world and the race continues.

Humanity is in a rush, and eager to cut corners. We've created mechanisms to ensure products don't last like Planned Obsolescence, where products are designed to stop working or require replacement at a certain point in time. Our cultures have adopted judgmental views that put pressure on us to be the first to have or do something. We're tired, stressed out, and wearing out. But what exactly are we rushing toward? When does the race end? What is "enough," and when?

I realized this behavior in myself early on in my career. At first, I wasn't making enough money to have the life I wanted. I was renting a room for a relatively extortionate price, leasing a cheap and unimpressive car, and couldn't afford things right away. I knew that if I kept on working hard, proved myself, and delivered results, I was going to get raises, promotions, and bonuses that would help me get the money I needed to be happy.

This created urgency within me. I wanted stuff "now," and the idea of saving the money I needed seemed more unobtainable than earning it through work. This started my creative engines and the drive to innovate flowed through me. The better, faster, and more impactful I could be, the more I would be recognized and, therefore, better rewarded financially. This approach worked but like the markets I was serving, competition was fierce. I had to be more innovative and impactful than those around me if I was going to continue being considered and rewarded. And, here's where the survival instincts kicked in. If somebody else beat me to the punch, I would be made redundant, demoted, or simply kept put. Others would surpass me, leaving me in their dust. Eventually, they would all be so far ahead, I would never be able to catch up. God help me if that was ever to happen.

I worked harder and faster. My survival depended on it. My behavior within my company and life mirrored the mechanics and viciousness of the wider system. I was competing against my colleagues in the same way my organization competed against the market. And in the process, my vision only went as far as it needed to. I didn't think of the consequences of my actions. I followed protocol and procedure, and as long as the powers that be approved of my actions, I was in the clear. The saddest part of this short-sighted way of working was that I did so at the expense of my own mental and physical health. What started as a genuine need to survive quickly turned into a constant hunger for "more." Years into my career, when I began earning a decent salary and could afford all the things I initially wanted, I was in debt and in a perpetual state of stress, driven by a rejuvenated need to survive. The more I earned, the more complex and demanding my work became. My lifestyle and "needs" also grew exponentially, and I found myself constantly in need of something. I was miserable, anxious, and my health was suffering. And, the worst part, I still didn't know what I was racing toward. When was enough, enough? I still didn't know.

I was being propelled forward by an unknown force. It was overwhelmingly powerful, and not being in forward motion all the time made me panic. I spent years unable to take a vacation without working. I couldn't enjoy a single weekend without cooking up new business ideas or working on a new project. I would regularly read and talk about "growth." Personal growth, professional growth, spiritual growth. Moving forward, moving upwards. If I wasn't moving, I was sinking. That's how I saw it, anyway, as many people around me did.

With the birth of my first daughter, and my struggle through the minefield of chemicals, toxins, pollutants, and other harm I had to constantly protect her from, I finally realized why things were the way they were. We are all moving forward so quickly, so ruthlessly, so selfishly, that we don't leave time to consider the consequences of our actions beyond the absolute minimum. There's no time to do it any other way.

Companies have legal and regulatory departments to set restrictions governing operational safety, but quite often these are limited to the minimum required by law. These boundaries are invisible lines we're told not to cross, but they're as fluid as their consequence. The harsher the consequences, and the more strictly they're enforced, the more effective those boundaries are. In the corporate world, however, there's often plenty of leeway. Think of sugar. It's a highly addictive substance with direct and proven consequences to human health, and despite the strict regulations around its inclusion in food, manufacturers always find a way to do so. They develop new forms of sugar, manipulate serving sizes and apply other tactics to keep their food addictive and dopamine-rewarding.

As we race toward an unknown, unachievable finish line, at an unprecedented speed, with the least possible ground rules—we're getting deeper and deeper into trouble. Within a matter of a few generations, we've already polluted our planet to the point of criticality. We've destroyed our forests, farming lands, oceans, and rivers, and plastered our beautiful landscapes in concrete.

We constantly pat our own backs, all the while turning a blind eye to the irreparable damage that we're causing ourselves. A great example of this is how proud we are of our extended lifespans. We live longer lives now than the generations before us, and revel in the technological and societal marvels that allowed us to achieve this.

But living longer doesn't mean living better. We're arguably dying of more avoidable and needless causes than ever. We're eating, drinking, smoking, and stressing ourselves into sickness. Our technologies and medical advances allow us to maintain life in spite of sickness, but that's not the same thing as living. We should be questioning these fundamentals, setting ourselves and future generations up for success, rather than applauding each other at every turn.

Welcome to the Era of Mindlessness, where accomplishing more trumps accomplishing better. Where today is all that counts. Where we keep fighting for survival, in spite of the abundance we have, against invisible and self-created threats. Where we are willing to burn ourselves out and sacrifice our minds and bodies to accomplish more. Where tomorrow's generation doesn't matter.

3. State of the World

Looking at the scroll of news headlines, it's hard not to be a cynic. The media loves to sensationalize everything, but the reality underneath it all is just as troubling. We've built this global economic system that is incredibly complex. The average person understands very little of it, yet our entire lives are shaped by, governed by, and in service of this system.

Our global political systems are just as complicated. The geopolitical landscape is vast, complex, fragmented, and highly volatile. It's hard enough for the average person to understand their own country's political system nowadays, let alone global institutions such as the United Nations, Interpol and numerous others that have sworn to protect the world in collaborative and universal fashion. The same can be said for healthcare, agriculture, education, and many of our most crucial industries. The world has grown and these industries, quite logically, have as well. But in our obsession with growth, sophistication, power, wealth, and dominance, many of these global systems are now corrupt, imbalanced and, at worst, destroying the world in sometimes unobvious and treacherous ways.

There's a time and place for celebration, and while there's plenty to celebrate in today's plethora of advancements and marvels, this isn't the time to do so. We're the only species that congregates to praise itself, and we're often blinded by our habitual self-praise. Social Media is a great example of how our blindness can get the better of us.

Ponder this for a moment: what has been social media's greatest impact on humanity? You might say something along the lines of fundamentally changing how we connect with others or reshaping the marketing landscape. And while these accomplishments are certainly profound, I credit social media's greatest contribution to something else.

I remember a time when the idea of disclosing your real name or anything about your personal identity online was preposterous. We used email addresses with cute nicknames and humorous innuendos. We would use cartoon avatars and fake locations. But it wasn't long before popular social networks began to bring about a sense of safety, making people feel more comfortable with being real online.

I credit Social Media with single-handedly changing the global perspective on privacy. It suddenly felt safe to disclose your name and photo to virtually the whole world—but not just one photo, many photos, along with your personal history, connections, and so much more. Very quickly, it became normal to post everything you did online. With cleverly crafted algorithms to keep us addicted, we gave away our privacy without a second thought so quickly that by the time any of us realized how exposed we were, it was too late. Our data was set free, the heels of our addictions dug in, and we became way too invested to let go.

This is what happens when big systems, big players, and an obsession with speed take over. The damage comes quickly, and by the time we wake up, it's too late.

From God-Made to Man-Made Food

We used to eat food. Delicious, nutritious food. Food that grew on trees and in the ground. We were free to roam the world and forage, eating what was available to us, with relatively little concern.

Fast forward just a century or so, and the nutritious, natural foods we once easily identified and found in nature are replaced by cans, jars, packets, boxes, and tins, each filled with the resemblance of what we once considered food.

Most people don't realize how dangerous our food has become. We've detached what we eat from its outcome. We've forgotten that we are, quite literally, what we eat. The food we consume contains the array of nutrients we need to flourish. But modern-day manufacturing processes, which cater to our hurried lives, have replaced these magnificent and essential-to-life components of food with chemicals, additives, preservatives, hormones, antibiotics, and genetically modified ingredients. These replacements, along with our obsession with fast food and sugary snacks, and stagnant modern lifestyle, have leap-frogged us into a pandemic of pandemics. Heart disease, diabetes, cancer, and an endless array of preventable diseases wipe out millions of lives each year.

People are dying needlessly and very often because of the food they eat. Let that sink in for a moment. The food we eat… is killing us.

That which is meant to give us life is now taking it away. What's more frightening is the fact that the vast majority of us are oblivious or, at the very least, indifferent to this problem.

Many people can't be blamed for not knowing. Most of us are born into a world of supermarkets, grocery stores, butcheries and bakeries. We know nothing about foraging in the wild, nor have access to it. Aisles and deli counters are our "wild," and the food we purchase for money or credit is our foraging. But then again, we do have access to information. We may not be to blame for creating the system, but are we not guilty for our choice to support it?

How many people do you know who would eat a fast-food burger or some deep-fried chicken, knowing that it's unhealthy, but choosing to ignore that fact? How many times have you opted for that super-large cola, extra-buttery popcorn, or extra-gooey chocolate bar knowing that you'll regret it the very next day? These are simple examples, but common ones that tend to reflect the majority of our daily food choices.

But why do we do this to ourselves? If we know better, why do it?

One main driver for this ignorant behavior is the fact that food companies spend billions of dollars each year marketing their products and confusing us in the process. They bombard us with tantalizing imagery, confusing messages, and misleading health claims. They dance on the borders of the legally permissible, kicking up so much dust in the process that none of us know what to believe anymore.

The dairy industry, for example, has been promoting the consumption of milk as part of a healthy diet for decades. They've claimed, and spent billions convincing us, that drinking milk is crucial to bone health. However, studies have demonstrated that the consumption of today's mass-produced cow juice may contribute to numerous diseases, including osteoporosis.[*] Let that one sink in as well. The food promoted to prevent osteoporosis contributes to the development of osteoporosis. Who are we supposed to believe? The scientists and researchers making these claims seemingly without moral bias, or the industry that refutes these claims with their own research? Are we supposed to simply forget decades of relentless marketing and adopt a new approach? What if they got it wrong? What if milk does contribute to healthy bones? What if the opposition is biased in ways we are yet to discover?

Food companies not only aim to sell as much as possible, but to profit as much as possible as well. To do this, they need to cut costs. Cutting costs commonly means cutting corners and finding cheaper options. But when it comes to food, are these tactics in the best interests of the consumer?

For example, artificial flavoring reduces the need for real, more expensive ingredients, but some are known to contribute to the development of disease. Food companies rely on regulators to hold them back. They follow the laws, stay within limits, and lobby for legal change when it benefits them.

---

[*]Milk Intake and Risk of Mortality and Fractures in Women and Men: Cohort Studies. https://www.ncbi.nlm.nih.gov/pmc/articles/PMC4212225/. Accessed 12 July 2021.

With billions of dollars injected into our economies each year by these companies, lawmakers tend to be wary of hindering or stifling them. It is a complex and intricate system, way out of reach for most of us.

Between the cost-saving shortcuts, relentless marketing, confusing messages, misleading claims, and profit-favoring lobbying, many of us are left frustrated and confused, often choosing ignorance because it's the easier path to follow.

From Healthcare to Sick Care

With poor diets, chemical-laden food and increasingly sedentary lifestyles, hundreds of millions of people are left fighting for their lives each year. While we marvel at the lifespans we are now capable of living, we neglect to realize that the quality of our last decades of life is increasingly rife with discomfort, disability, and disease.

We've become obsessed with quick solutions. In keeping up with our race toward the future, we have become averse to struggle and strife. Our bodies are built to withstand stress and strain, yet we've come to fear the discomfort that used to have a purpose and place in human health. Just as exposure to viruses and bacteria can strengthen our immune systems, so can physical exertion and exposure to the elements. In today's world, however, we've become comfortable living in luxury, and demand from our healthcare providers that they remove any pain or discomfort without delay.

Humans used to be able to take care of themselves. We were versed in natural treatments and remedies, and able to manage our own basic health needs.

We turned to those skilled in medicine and healthcare when we faced illnesses we were unable to tend to ourselves.

Today we've become complacent in our self-care. We seek out quick-acting remedies and no longer have patience. We're seemingly unable to tolerate the most minor health issues. Even the minor head or stomach ache is immediately remedied with over-the-counter medication containing chemicals with implications we know nothing about. We pop pills, drink formulas, and numb ourselves without any concern for consequence. Stopping the discomfort is our priority.

The healthcare system once favored the healthy. It was built to bring solutions to problems the average person was unable to resolve themselves. Doctors and nurses treated their patients with care and concern, and getting to the root of the problem was the priority. If we were able to identify the cause, we could prevent the problem from occurring again.

Healthcare has now evolved into "sick care," and profit is driven by the ill. Remedying symptoms takes precedence over resolving root causes, and patients have become commodities in an industry worth trillions.

But who's to blame for such a corrupt system? Is it the hospitals, practitioners, pharmaceutical companies, or educational institutions? It's easy to point a finger at the big, bad machine. We use names like "Big Pharma" to incite fear toward a large, mysterious and devious enemy. But the truth is that most of us have some share in the blame. While there certainly are companies out there that behave maliciously and take advantage of unwitting and innocent people, quite often they're just giving us more of what we demand. Each person who prefers quick fixes to long-term solutions or refuses to educate themselves on their bodies and the medicines they take is to blame. Every person who rushes to the drugstore and blindly purchases medicines rather than tolerate a little pain is to blame. Every one of us who allows hospitals and clinics to turn us into commodities rather than treat us with care and respect and allow us the time to feel listened to and cared for is to blame. We all play a role in contributing to this feedback loop.

From Progression to Regression

Our choices shape the world economy. Every purchase or payment is a vote. It's an acknowledgment that we're okay with what's provided. It's the reason the healthcare system is the way it is—we vote with our complacent participation, our payments and our acceptance of the way things are. And the same goes for virtually every industry.

Since the start of the twenty-first century, our lives have very rapidly been taken over by technology. Actually, that statement is misleading. Technology hasn't taken over our lives, but rather *we've invited it into our lives*. In any case, the change has indeed been rapid, leaving most people with little to no idea as to how the technologies they are so dependent on work.

Our homes, offices and vehicles are interlaced with hundreds (if not thousands) of electronic devices and gadgets. We carry them in our pockets and purses. We place them on, and even inside, our bodies. We sleep with them near our heads. We eat with them at our tables. We hold them, stare at them, touch them, and even love them.

We've become dependent on them, addicted to them. They've transformed humanity; changing the way we operate, communicate, and live. But how much do we understand about them, really?

In any intimate relationship, you get to know a person before you move in with them, marry them, or invest in them. Yet with the technologies we have so intrusively welcomed into the most intimate parts of our lives, we do very little to get to understand them.

Consider mobile phones. If we were any more attached to them, they would be surgically implanted. There's a pandemic of smartphone addiction, and it has even begun affecting children as young as two or three years old. We use them daily and rely on them for almost all our communication. They dominate our personal lives and are arguably the most critical parts of our work lives. Without them we are isolated from the world, disconnected from our friends and families, vulnerable, and literally lost without the aid of the features, functionalities, and a plethora of apps that have replaced effort with convenience. But again, most people know nothing about them. For example, besides the occasional conspiracy theories that pop-up on our social feeds, most of us know very little about how radio frequency radiation really works[†] or how it impacts the body.

We're not aware of the level of mental or physical damage staring at a small screen for several hours a day can cause.[‡]

[†]Radiofrequency (RF) Radiation. https://www.cancer.org/cancer/cancer-causes/radiation-exposure/radiofrequency-radiation.html Accessed 28 Feb. 2021.
[‡]Screen-Time Is Associated with Inattention Problems in

We don't question the separation and social damage caused by our smartphone addictions* and even fewer actually do anything about it. Between the fear of missing out and the very practical reasons to not want to completely disconnect from the world, curbing this very challenging issue takes real, collective effort. But once again, ignorance is bliss and requires much less work.

Our addictions and dependence on our phones, as well as the complex technologies and infrastructure needed to give us what we want, have made us vulnerable. We're in a state of need and the powers that provide can essentially do what they want. We've voted. We've told them what we want and they will continue to feed our gluttonous desires for more. We want smarter phones, faster connection speeds, lower latency, more apps, better cameras, and they will happily oblige in return for our monetary votes.

The problem with this seemingly simple and mutually beneficial relationship is that we don't know what goes into providing us with what we demand. The materials that make up our devices and gadgets, the chemicals used in production processes, the logistics involved, and the environmental impact of distribution—they're not simple. Often, they're intertwined with competitive defensiveness and corporate secrecy. Everything that goes into our beloved devices is essentially kept in a black box. Ignorance may sometimes be

---

Preschoolers: Results from the CHILD Birth Cohort Study. https://www.journals.plos.org/plosone/article?id=10.1371%2Fjournal.pone.0213995 Accessed 28 Feb. 2021.
*Trends on Tuesday: People Are Crazy about Mobile! – Digital. Gov. https://digital.gov/2013/08/13/trends-on-tuesday-people-arecrazy-about-mobile/ Accessed 28 Feb. 2021

bliss, but in this case, the contents of this box have real consequences to our health, environment, and humanity at large. These consequences are tangible and may be a threat to commercial interests if exposed or widely understood.

The reason for this goes back to our voting dollars. Every cent spent (or not spent) determines a company's commercial success or failure. If we truly understood the risks of many of the products we so casually and haphazardly consume, we might avoid them like the plague. Our not knowing serves commercial interests, as well as our own and so many of us are happy to remain ignorant of the possibilities. In many cases we know exactly what the consequences of our choices are, yet we're willing to turn a blind eye.

The relationship between consumer and company is complex. We need them, and they need us. Many will jump to pointing the finger at large corporations for their actions, or governments for their inactions, but the truth is, these organizations aren't machines with minds of their own. They're made up of people, humans like you and me. They think and feel, sweat and bleed. They make choices, as do we. Collectively, these choices influence each other. The people working in these corporate and governmental organizations take a step in a particular direction, and we respond with a step either toward or away from them and vice-versa. Each one of us plays a role in this relationship and its outcome is a shared responsibility.

The End of an Era

It's troubling to realize how much diligence is required to remain safe in today's world. From the environmental toxins we're exposed to, to the risks and potential dangers posed by our telecommunications infrastructure (both of which are virtually inescapable and invisible), there's an increasing amount of diligence required to stay healthy and safe. At the speed we're moving, particularly concerning technology, the risks are only going to increase. It's not enough to consider things in isolation. Everything influences everything else. Perhaps a particular chemical or technology isn't harmful in isolation. But bring poor diets, sedentary lifestyles, environmental toxins, chronic stress, and the numerous other factors that fill our lives into consideration, and it may just be the tipping point.

4. The River We Live Upon

Imagine living on the bank of a river. You have a beautiful house overlooking a gorgeous view of mountainous terrain. You live at peace, sourcing your food from the nature surrounding you. Your water supply is fresh, cleansed through nature's own filtration process and endlessly abundant.

One day, as you enjoy a bath in the river, you notice the water changing color, from clear blue to a hazy crimson. It appears to be blood, coming from upstream. It's no longer safe for you and your family to bathe in or drink, so you investigate. As you trek upstream, hunting for the source of the contamination, you arrive at a new settlement. Several houses sit along the riverbank, and among them, a slaughterhouse. They've craftily positioned it at the end of the settlement so that the blood washes downstream, leaving them with fresh, uncontaminated water to bathe in and drink.

You approach the owner of the slaughter-house and explain to them your dilemma. Your water is being contaminated by their facility and your family can no longer rely on the river. They tell you they can't do anything and send you on your way. Disheartened by the situation, you vow to find a solution. Water, after all, is crucial for survival. And your family's survival is your utmost priority. Moving your house isn't an option, and building a new one is too time-consuming and laborious. You make claim to some land beyond the new settlement and begin barreling fresh water. These barrels are then brought to your home, and your problem seems to be resolved. The process, however, is tedious and expensive, and long-term viability soon becomes a concern. You can't handle the extra labor on your own, and you can't afford to hire someone else.

However, you soon learn that there are other houses further downstream facing the same issue as yourself. Their once pristine water supply has now become tainted, and you see an opportunity to help them and yourself. You have the advantage of being closer to the slaughterhouse and have already set up a barreling facility upstream. So, you begin selling barrels of clean water to those living downstream.

At first, you sell each barrel for a small price—just enough to cover the costs of a few employees and the barrels themselves. But as your business begins to grow, you realize you don't need to barrel water for yourself anymore, you can afford to build a new house much further upstream. You and your family now have a thriving business, a brand-new house, and are back to drinking and bathing in fresh water. As you live your new and almost self-sustaining life, you realize there's an opportunity to help others. You buy out the land for miles upstream and begin building houses. You sell them at a premium because of the clean water. As this new community begins to develop, you realize yet another opportunity to help. The growing population needs to eat meat, so you build a slaughterhouse of your own.

Not wanting to pollute the water of your own community, you place it at the end of the settlement, so that the contaminants wash downstream. As you and your neighbors thrive, the houses further away continue to suffer even more. Focused on your own family, survival, flourishing businesses and responsibilities toward your own community, you've become removed from the problems of those living further downstream.

This story demonstrates something that I believe has become the driving force behind the Era of Mindlessness that we currently live in: being untouched by the consequences of our actions. As long as the results of our actions are deferred, physically distant, and cannot be traced back to us, it's easy to choose blissful ignorance. To keep a firm grip on our modern comforts, ignorance is the luxury we bank on but can no longer afford.

When you lived downstream, the sudden contamination of your once-flawless water supply was incredibly disruptive. The results of other people's actions were very real to you and your family, but when you moved upstream and began resolving your troubles, you became further and further removed from the consequences of other people's actions and, eventually, your own. The moral of the story is: the further away we are from a problem, the less we're concerned with it.

As we enjoy the luxuries we're born into, little do we think about the consequences of our actions. In today's complex commercial landscape, the processes involved in producing, distributing, and stocking our food, water and other essentials keep us blinded from any collateral damage.

We have to see through layers upon layers of information, and have the added challenge of being blinded and having the truth skewed by the manufactures and endless companies involved along the way.

It's not easy to understand or see what's happening downstream anymore. We're no longer living on the riverbank and our problems aren't as simple as they once were. The impacts of our consumption and waste-management decisions are methodically, meticulously, and deliberately kept from us. This distance is to our advantage. We don't have the time, resources or capabilities needed to deal with the by-products. Imagine how complex and tiresome life would be if we all had to deal with our own garbage, food and water supplies, and everything else that supports our modern and luxurious lives.

Don't get me wrong, there's a lot to appreciate, a lot to enjoy and a lot to marvel at. Society has progressed thanks to innovation across virtually every industry. Basic human needs are handed to us on silver platters, and we're able to focus on so much more. We're no longer occupied by basic survival needs and we can begin working our way up the hierarchy of needs. At the top of this pyramid is self-actualization; a state of enlightenment and realization that some might argue is the pinnacle of human existence. And it is thanks to the brain-work and labor of countless people over the last century that has paved the way for us.

Everything has its price though. It would be foolish for any of us to think that the luxury and conveniences we are provided come for free. There is always a price to pay, and this time it's the price of deliberate effort. Because we're so far removed from the work and processes involved in providing us with virtually everything, the consequences of our actions and decisions are no longer blatantly obvious, as was the blood flowing down the river once upon a time. We now need to make a deliberate and conscious effort to see what's happening downstream if this Era of Mindlessness is going to come to an end.

This will take some serious effort and will almost certainly disrupt our lives. That is, however, if we approach it haphazardly. With a system in place to guide our thinking and remind us of how and what to do, we can build a new mindset that eventually becomes second nature to us. We can teach it in schools and at home, apply it at work or in our personal lives, and perhaps save those downstream.

If you think about the river in our story earlier as representing time, then the people living downstream are the generations to come. They are our children and grandchildren, who will pay the biggest price for the consequences of our actions, as we did those of our parents and grandparents.

There are also immediate consequences to our actions. Air pollution is a real and ongoing concern. The tons of plastic and other waste contaminating our oceans and water supplies are real and ongoing concerns, as is child labor, the toxins in our food and other products, and so much more.

There are millions upon millions of people suffering as a consequence of others getting to inhabit this modern, luxurious world. While a new mindset would certainly benefit people today, the further removed population are the people yet to be born. The worst outcomes of today's problems are yet to show themselves. Those of us alive today may be lucky enough to no longer be here when it really hits the fan. But our children will begin to pay a hefty price, and their children even more, unless, of course, we change the path we're on.

5. Ending the Era of Mindlessness

To bring an end to this Era of Mindlessness, one might argue that it's as simple as learning to become more mindful. Mindfulness is a practice that stems from Buddhist traditions but has made its way into the world of psychology and Western spirituality. Recently, and thanks to technology, a wide variety of mindfulness practices have emerged, becoming accessible to the masses. It is now a fairly widely understood concept. Mindfulness is no more complicated than being present in the moment, focused on what is happening right now, rather than what has occurred or what may occur. But admittedly, it's a lot easier said than done.

In formal practice, mindfulness requires discipline. It's also quite difficult to compete with everything else in our lives that demands our attention. These days, most of us are chronically distracted and lead demanding and busy lives. Many people struggle to eat mindfully, inhaling their food between meetings, chores, and outings. Living in this fast-paced world, it takes some serious effort to slow things down, particularly mentally, and we tend to miss out on a great deal of detail along the way. Think of the wholesome apple. Often touted as a quick and easy snack, it's also a great source of nutrition. However, in a quick grab-and-go moment, we may scarf it down without any real consideration for what it is that we're eating. In this seemingly ordinary fruit is a lot to admire and appreciate.

Each of the thousands of different types of apples in existence has its own unique color, flavor, and texture. They are all chock-full of vitamins, minerals, and phytonutrients, hydrating and nourishing our bodies. Their seeds can sprout to form large trees that provide us wood for shelter and paper, and branches and leaves for shade and protection. These small fruits are so beautifully crafted and fit ever so snugly in our hands, almost as if they were made for us. They're beautifully fragrant, delicious and can be included in so many dishes. From salads to hot desserts, they go so well with so many other ingredients. It's incredible how much this tiny fruit has to offer, but most of us have never stopped to marvel at its finer qualities.

Mindfulness allows us to notice such details, which can then bring deeper understanding and appreciation of these numerous blessings. Doing so, however, requires us to slow things down and become more deliberate in our actions—a vital skill if we're going to end the mindless behavior we are so unnaturally and programmatically inclined toward.

Obviously, it's difficult to be mindful all of the time, but the practice can open our eyes and minds to the intricacies and beauty of life. It allows us to take things into consideration that we may normally not. For example, our interactions can be substantially elevated when we're in a mindful state. In being mindful with one another, we can access greater empathy and compassion. We can notice the finer details in expression, tone, and feeling, all of which allude to unspoken truths, creating deeper understanding and connection. It's a powerful tool, yet one that is easily and quickly overruled and overrun by today's modern and addictive distractions, and our race toward the future.

So, if mindfulness is a logical solution to end our mindlessness, how are we supposed to break through the mental clutter and muster up the effort needed to become more mindful? Well, there's a concept in neuroscience called neuroplasticity, which states that the human brain can be "rewired," essentially allowing a person to develop new behaviors.

Think of habits. You're not born with them. You develop them, and they can be changed. This also applies to our thought processes. In the same way you learned a method for thinking and making decisions, you can unlearn that method and replace it with another. In this case, one that has better outcomes. Through regular practice over time, we can learn to make more mindful choices. To do this we need a specific method to practice with. One that is both systematic and easily replicable so that we can remain consistent over time. The end result: replacing a mindless practice with a mindful one.

Mindful Futurism is a simple framework that guides and restructures our thinking, allowing us to become more mindful in our decisions. Think of it as a template that can be applied to virtually any decision in life. With the vast number of decisions we have to make each day, we need a crutch to lean on that's efficient and versatile, eventually achieving this mental rewiring that needs to happen for mindful decision-making to become second nature to us.

Having a common framework allows us to easily share it with others and communicate our application of it. It unifies us in a common practice that can be built upon and improved over time. Mindful Futurism is simple, easy to apply and combines several familiar concepts into one practical approach that aims to shift humanity into a better trajectory. It's not meant to compete against or replace other similar practices but complement and support them through the provision of a universal methodology.

Mindful Futurism is a belief system that encourages the deliberate and mindful consideration of the well-being, safety and security of all forms of life, with the intention of building a better future for the next generation.

It requires a shift in thinking, where the consideration of future implications is given priority over short-term outcomes when making decisions.

To build a foundational understanding, let's break the premise down into smaller pieces and go into some depth as to their value and contribution:

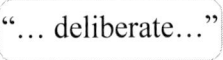

"… deliberate…"

When we are at our busiest, we often switch to auto-pilot—drifting through a period of time in a preoccupied, or perhaps mindless, state. In this state, we are detached from the present moment and don't think through our decisions. Some are automatically triggered based on habit or external motivation. Others are done without preprogrammed behavioral patterns and are results of anticipation or simply a lack of awareness. In either case, we're not always thinking things through as thoroughly as we normally would and certainly wouldn't give extra consideration to the present.

Being deliberate, as part of Mindful Futurism, is intended to ensure that the decisions we make are thought through. They're not results of mindless execution or instinctive reactions, but exacted and precise consideration. The goal here is to look back on our decisions and remove the possible excuses of "I didn't realize" or "that's how it's always done."

Every opportunity in life is an opportunity to change. We can change our beliefs and decisions. Every moment brings with it an opportunity to change the course that we are on. Through deliberateness, we are conscious of the fact that we have chosen our path, and leave no room for excuses or deflection.

> "… mindful…"

Mindfulness, by its most common definition, requires us to focus on the present moment, stripping away any distractions and centering our energy and attention on something specific. In this state, we can focus, think clearly and return our thoughts to the matter at hand if we suddenly find ourselves drifting away.

Mindfulness is also being deliberate in our decision-making. It's an essential partner in the process, ensuring we are focused not only on the present moment, but those to come as well. It is taking into account the magnitude, or lack thereof, of what has been presented to us, and on this basis, acting with purpose and caution.

> "... consideration of the well-being, safety, and security..."

In this mindful state, we want to pay attention to a few critical elements. The first is the well-being of others, which can be broken down into physical, mental, and spiritual well-being. Each of us can impact all of these elements within each other. We should aspire to do no harm to the physicality of others—whether directly or indirectly. We should be concerned for the mental well-being of our fellow humans, ensuring we cause them no distress nor grief. And, we should allow our fellow brothers and sisters to find their ways through life freely and unhindered.

Whether it's as a parent, sibling, friend, colleague, or neighbor, most of us have some kind of responsibility for the safety and security of others. The amount of responsibility varies according to the type of relationship, but the importance of ensuring the safety and security of others is always important. In Mindful Futurism, those with power, influence, or the ability to impact the lives of others, have the greatest levels of responsibility. "With great power comes great responsibility," as the saying goes and we should apply our concerns for those alive today, as well as those to follow.

> "...all forms of life..."

We value our own above all else—that's both understandable and universal to all living things. We value our species over others, our families over others, our children over others. In Mindful Futurism, it is about going beyond this limited thinking and having consideration for all living things. While there are moments and challenges in life that warrant preference of one group over another, these are few and far between compared to all the opportunities we have to connect and help others. This also extends our consideration beyond life, to its most essential components. It creates an inclusive mindset where we recognize the criticality of our water, food supplies, environment each other and all living things.

We're all interconnected—dependent on each other for sustenance, survival and even comfort. Every living thing contributes to and is dependent on this global ecosystem within which we live. Even the stars and planets around us play a critical role in the survival of our species. Every element within this system of systems has its place, beautifully and masterfully positioned to give and take in precise amounts. All forms of life, therefore, are equally important and vital to our own existence.

> "... intention of building a better future for the next generation."

There is nothing wrong with wanting to innovate, progress, or improve.

It comes part and parcel with our humanity as we move up the hierarchy of needs toward the peak of worldly possibility. The modern-day charge toward the future, however, is often misplaced, corrupted by ego or greed, or simply left without predefined intention. Through applying intention to our desires for bigger, better, stronger, and sooner, we can put our egos in check and unite our efforts for greater impact.

The Baby Boomers and their parents were arguably responsible for some of the most wide-reaching and life-altering innovations in documented history. For the first time, mankind was able to overcome the physical limitations of our world reaching virtually every corner of the earth, and even breach our atmosphere in search of extraterrestrial success. Through their daring ventures and ground-breaking pursuits, however, they introduced a plethora of environmental, sociological, geopolitical, economic and health related challenges that the generations to follow would not only adopt, but be left to suffer the consequences of.

Our choices and actions today will certainly impact the lives of those who follow, as did those of our parents and grandparents and theirs before them. By focusing our intentions on the next generation, we are honoring and respecting our natural responsibilities as predecessors. With Mindful Futurism, we are going one step further and not just intending to "do no harm" but to do "even better." We intend to relieve our children and grandchildren from the woes that we adopted and allow them every opportunity to flourish in ways we were not. There is a greater purpose beyond ourselves assigned to our daily efforts and decisions.

The Three Principles

Mindful Futurism is anchored by three core principles:

The First Principle: Accept Responsibility

> "We must accept full responsibility for the actions we take, even those taken on behalf, or upon the orders, of others."

Regardless of why we do what we do, one thing is undoubted: we are each responsible for our own actions. Perhaps in some rare circumstance can we alleviate all responsibility for a particular choice, but for the most part, we have to accept our role as the performer of the action and therefore bear the responsibility. Very commonly, particularly in the business world, we do things because we're told to. It's easy for a person to assume that since they're such a small cog in "the machine," that their choices don't matter. Our survival instincts may be highly activated, and doing what's expected or asked of us to keep our job, protect our career, and maintain our income takes priority over anything else. The need to survive kicks in and we adopt a victim-like mentality: "I need this job; therefore, I have to do what I'm told; therefore, I am innocent of the action I've taken."

While this vulnerable position is completely understandable, and relatable to many, it's little more than self-deception. We are almost always presented with a choice. Whether it's simply to propose another way or completely resign ourselves from the responsibility itself—we always have a choice.

As the maker of this choice, we must accept that the consequences are owed to us alone. The driving force to achieve this will be to adopt a more rebellious mindset—not a dysfunctional or disruptive one, but a healthy rebellion against our own mental and emotional limitations. We need to put our worldly fears aside, push back, and act like the conscious beings that we are.

The Second Principle: Acknowledge Impact

> "We must acknowledge that our actions have the potential to affect the wellbeing, safety and security of all forms of life."

Adopting this thinking brings more importance to every decision we make. We can no longer hide behind other people or circumstances and must face the future head-on. In doing so, we apply healthy pressure on ourselves that elevates us to a higher state of consciousness. It also brings us one step closer to the people downstream, who will most certainly be impacted in some way by the choices we make.

If you're thinking, "one small decision can't make enough of a difference to warrant all of this effort," think of your influence on the course of history as a minor shift in the aiming of a gun. A slight offset of the gun's sights will result in a potentially significant shift in the trajectory of the bullet. The further away the target, the more noticeable this shift becomes. Parents understand this better than anyone, perhaps. Children are blank slates, and every decision a parent makes for them (no matter how small) shapes and reshapes their mental, emotional, physical, and even spiritual world. Children adopt the most subtle and subconscious influences. The attitude of a friend, the mannerisms of a favorite relative, the ideals of a teacher. They're sponges and every interaction, event, or experience wets that sponge.

Although we may not have this level of influence in every situation, each of us has a significant role to play in this world. And, as the Butterfly Effect suggests, something as seemingly insignificant as the flap of a butterfly's wings can contribute to the development of a tornado. No matter how far removed our decisions may feel from the lives of others, a ripple effect of consequences occurs and the result may certainly be life-altering in some way.

The Third Principle: Act Deliberately

> "We must make informed decisions, and do our best to ensure a positive outcome for future generations."

Most of our decisions are based on assumptions, precedents, traditions, or simply the instructions of others. We make choices without really understanding why things are done in certain ways, or what the outcomes may be. In the corporate world, processes and standard operating procedures tend to replace independent thinking. Although there is plenty of logic behind building on the work and knowledge of others, we shouldn't put aside our own curiosities and due diligence. At the very least, we should question why things are done in a particular way. We shouldn't turn a blind eye, just because someone smarter told us to do something.

A great example of this is in healthcare. It's very common for patients to feel that medical doctors always know better. Although doctors are experts in their fields and know the intricacies of their specializations better than most people, we shouldn't completely dismiss how much we know about our own bodies. You may not be a doctor, but you are certainly an expert in yourself. You also have the cognitive ability to ask questions, and at the very least try your best to understand how a particular diagnosis was awarded or why a certain prescription was written. The point here is to make an effort toward understanding and asking the right questions, so that you walk out knowing more than you did walking in.

This line of thinking can be applied to virtually any situation. Whether it is at work, at home, or at school, we have every right to ask questions, challenge ideas, and propose alternatives. Within the concept of Mindful Futurism, this approach is a necessary part of taking full responsibility for our actions. Through researching, intellectualizing and contemplating, we can execute our decisions with confidence and lessen the likelihood of making avoidable mistakes. Applying this with the conscious and deliberate effort toward building positive outcomes for future generations, we potentially have a formula for success.

The Three Steps

Sometimes, the simplest solutions are the most powerful ones. Mindful Futurism is meant to be just that: simple. It's not some philosophical breakthrough that's meant to stimulate thought without action. It's meant to be a practical, straightforward solution to a very real problem.

Our lives and lifestyles have a strong grasp on our behaviors and intentions, and breaking through requires a lifeline, something we can firmly hold onto, go back to, or turn to in our weakest times. This lifeline consists of three simple steps, which can easily be remembered and applied in nearly any setting.

Step 1: Identifying Purpose

A person can spend an entire lifetime in search of their purpose. It's a North Star upon which we set our course in life and it keeps us steadfast through the most turbulent of times. By knowing where we're heading, we can remain aware of the events, decisions and people nudging us off-course. While identifying one's life purpose may be daunting, difficult, or even seem impossible to do, most of the decisions we make on a daily basis are a lot simpler to figure out once we have done so.

Before making any decision, try to understand the purpose behind it. If one doesn't exist, then explore options and identify one yourself. Without one, you run the risk of blindly following in the footsteps of others, or just making some mindless decision because one needs to be made.

No decision is too small to have a purpose. Even something as relatively inconsequential as buying a new pair of shoes deserves some consideration, and the more vital decisions certainly do. Every decision becomes a brick on the path ahead of us, and we need to know where we're heading. By identifying the aim we have, or the specific value we're seeking to gain, we can then find a mindful solution to meet that need.

Step 2: Apply Due Diligence

Routine decisions are usually made without being thought through. Life-altering decisions, and those involving money, however, do tend to be offered a fair amount of consideration. The goal here is to apply the same mindful approach to as many decisions as possible. We will need to perform a varying amount of due diligence in any given situation, understanding as much as we can about the circumstances, potential outcomes, alternatives, and so on. This effort and the knowledge obtained as an outcome of applying it gives us a bank of knowledge to take into Step 3.

Step 3: Make Your Decision

With a clearly identified purpose or intention and thorough consideration of the situation or opportunity at hand, you are equipped with what you need to take deliberate and effective action. You apply what you've learned and accept full responsibility for what you're about to execute. At this stage, you should feel content with the level of research, thinking, and feeling you've put into the process—whether it took a minute or a month.

Now, pull the trigger and trust that you've done the best you can to ensure that your decision will contribute to a better tomorrow.

These steps are straightforward, easy to remember and quite effortlessly applied. The real effort, however, goes into adopting the mindset that makes these three steps mean something. It's letting go of our addictions and ego and consciously caring for the generations to come, rather than continuing to saturate our minds, hearts and lives with worldly pleasures that benefit little more than ourselves. If you find yourself unsure of where to start, refer back to the Three Principles. They serve as the boundaries.

6. The Trodden Path

From an early age, we are taught to choose the trodden path—the one our parents took, and theirs before them. It is a safe path where you can find comfort in knowing that you are not alone on your journey through life.

Taking the trodden path serves a vital role in our existence as humans. It allows us to build upon the work and knowledge of others, innovate and, most importantly, survive. As children, we must follow in the footsteps of others. But, as we grow older and a little wiser, we find ourselves wanting to veer off on a course of our own. The early stages of this desire appear during our teenage years, as we begin to form a rebellion against the ways of the older generation. We develop a deep desire to explore and experiment and we eventually get the chance to do so.

At some point in our lives, commonly in our late teens or early twenties, we take our first meaningful steps into adulthood and begin to choose our own paths. This may be a first job, graduating from high-school, entering college, or getting married. It could be so many things, but the commonality is that this first step requires us to begin making decisions for ourselves.

We're no longer willing, or perhaps able, to continue following in the footsteps of our parents in the same way we did for so many years. We become men and women in our own rights, and suddenly the path ahead of us isn't as clear as it once was. It is both thrilling and frightening. But, at some point, we must accept this inevitable step in our existence and embrace whatever lies ahead.

The first few steps are always the most difficult. They are often the first big decisions we have to make for ourselves. And whether they involve deciding what classes to take, what company to join, or which person to marry, we must eventually push through the fear and make a choice.

As we grow older and begin to take on greater responsibilities, our decisions tend to become more critical and difficult to make. We may find ourselves responsible for other people—spouses, children, business partners, employees—and the risks associated with making the wrong decisions can begin to take a toll on our thinking and behavior. We learn to ask others for help and guidance, and quite often find ourselves comforted by the paths most trodden. We value the safety and security in the known, and, eventually, many of us consequently lose our sense of rebellion and adventure. We learn to play it safe, and to some extent find ourselves seeing value in the ways of our parents.

Our paths aren't as independent as we may think. Influences from all facets of our lives subtly nudge us in varying directions. "The norm" is often touted as being the "correct" way, and rebellion of any sort is often unwelcomed or advised against.

This makes veering off-course scarier and riskier, both of which go against our innate desire to remain close to others and survive.

As my old mentor said those years ago, "Real change happens when people do." We need to alter the path we are on for the better and the only way to do so is together. We must recognize and acknowledge the significance of our roles in each other's lives. We teach our children, advise our friends and colleagues, support our families, and set examples for others with our actions—all of which impact our collective path. We need to become more conscious of the interconnected web of influences in our lives and, by recognizing and choosing to no longer be blindly influenced by them, revive that rebellious and adventurous spirit within us.

As we trot through life, distracted by the experiences and challenges that come our way, it is easy to lose sight of the bigger picture. We make countless decisions, many of which are quite often made in spontaneity or urgency and we forget their significance and influence somewhere downstream. If we take a bird's eye view of our lives and trace back to the events or influences that led us to the choices we make, it is easier for us to see the bigger picture and our role within it.

To illustrate this, let us examine the career of a young woman. As you read through her story, notice the distractions in her life and how they influence her thinking. Challenge yourself to consider how her decisions impacted others, and what choices you would have made if you faced the same challenges and obstacles.

Case Study: "Free at Last"

Recently graduated, Amy was excited, youthfully ambitious and ready to take on the world. She quickly landed her first job interview with a large multinational corporation. On the day of the appointment, as she drove toward their head office, she began to imagine all the possibilities that lay before her. Working for a company of this caliber would be an honor, and look incredible on her resumé. She was lucky to have been given this opportunity, and she knew it.

While approaching the front doors, the pressure began to sink in. "I can't screw this up," she repeated over and over in her head, as she entered the lobby. Striding across the marble floor, the clacking of her footsteps echoed through the foyer as she approached the front desk, with the company logo printed proudly across it. She felt overwhelmed with the apparent power and magnificence. "I'm actually here," she muses giddily as she signs in. She heads to an elaborate waiting area, with rows of plush lounge chairs, restricted access doors, and awards hanging on the wall—further accentuating the company's global dominance and brand appeal—and takes a seat among an army of other candidates who, judging by their wide eyes and anxious smiles, all seem to be as dazzled and nervous as she is.

The exciting potential of working for a large brand, particularly one you know well or admire, can have a significant influence over your thoughts and emotions. Human Resource professionals often tap into behavioral science to design perks and packages, and even position brands, in ways that create a sense of exclusivity and pride in their employees. Often, we wear the brands we work for as badges of honor, and even proudly proclaim former affiliations (think Xoogler). The same can be said for university students, startup founders, performance artists, and even in marriage. We are intoxicated by the pride and excitement of our first big entry into adulthood and independence.

What moment or opportunity signified your entry into adulthood? What were your thoughts and feelings as you took those first steps?

> Her interview comes to a close after what feels like an eternity, but she handled it like a pro and she knows it. A life of independence and freedom now seems within reach. Her childhood dreams of buying and doing whatever she wanted in life are suddenly beginning to feel possible.
>
> She gets a call a few days later and is offered the job. As the initial excitement of this momentous opportunity settles, she begins to feel something strange—a newfound sense of freedom and maturity, shackles she was never aware of suddenly removed. With her arms and legs free at last, she could wander the world fully for the first time.

We tend to associate freedom with money. And the more of it we have, the freer we think we are. It's both ironic and sad that we associate our ability to purchase or possess material wealth with freedom. It's only when our mental or physical health is in question that we finally realize what freedom truly means. In the meantime, we surround ourselves with stuff and develop attachments to the things we work so hard to acquire. From childhood, this thinking is programmed into us. We emulate our parents, follow trends to fit in with our peers and become drowned by corrupt and manipulative advertising. By the time we enter adulthood, our thirst for this so-called freedom peaks, and our choices are often dictated or at the very least influenced by the seductive nature of money.

Do you remember your first paycheck? What did you feel? What did you buy? Have your views on money and material wealth changed over the years?

> As the months went by and Amy settled into her new life, she decided to buy a new car. A beautiful array of German cars, muscle cars, and SUVs lined the parking lot outside her office building. Everyone was fairly well paid, and it showed. Her clunky second-hand was no longer appropriate. She was "one of them," after all, and she needed to look the part.
>
> When she finally found a car she loved, she realized she was stretching herself financially. But she was making a decent salary, worked for a large and stable company, and had her whole life ahead of her to pay it off anyway.
>
> *People take out loans for a lot more and do just fine*, she thought to herself, and gleefully made the purchase.

Our financial systems have given us an incredible gift: the ability to live beyond our means. While the concept of loans dates back thousands of years, today's banking system makes it easier and more accessible than ever. From as early as our teen years, we can take out substantial loans, credit cards, and even mortgages, and while this privilege opens doors and creates opportunity, it comes to us years before most of us ever truly understand the value of money. Our addiction to stuff and the comfort it brings us, coupled with social pressure, media-driven influence, and "the dream" being so widely and aggressively sold to us, creates a powerful trap that many of us fall into very early in our lives.

What were your first big purchases? Did you spend within your means, or take out a loan or payment plan? In hindsight, how do you feel about those choices? What about your more recent purchasing behavior? Has it changed at all?

> As the months went by, work started to pick up and she began to feel the burn. It was hard work, but her excitement and the financial reward drove her forward.
>
> Over time, she began going to dinners and birthday gigs, forming bonds and turning her colleagues into trusted friends. Her life began to revolve around work now, but it didn't feel like work. It felt like home. She would go to sleep late and wake up early, work on the weekends and delay her holidays. She was buzzing with the responsibilities bestowed upon her and was constantly nudged forward through recognition and reward.

> Long hours, late nights, and short weekends became the norm. Amazingly, whenever she began to feel overwhelmed and could sense burnout quickly approaching, she would be given a raise or a promotion.

We're always told to "work hard," but what does that really mean? It often equates to how much we give our companies in return for our salaries. In the corporate world, how late a person stays at the office is often considered a reflection of their dedication and "hard work." In other jobs, it may be the number of hours worked or the number of transactions processed. In the startup world, it is quite common to find founders tout their lack of sleep and financial struggles as indicators of their commitment to their companies. The general tendency here is to suffer as a result of working hard. Now that this behavior is ingrained in corporate culture, it is a real challenge to break the mold and do things differently. Pacing ourselves, and working smarter rather than harder, is commonly seen as laziness or lack of commitment.

It is only after we reach our limits that we step off the path we're on, and onto another that is less self-destructive.

What does "working hard" mean to you? Do you recall a time in your professional life where you reached (or nearly reached) burnout? If so, what pushed you to your limit? How did you handle it? If you could go back and do things differently, what would you do?

> Two years went by and she was no longer the new kid on the block. She was a supervisor now and on her way to becoming the company's youngest manager. That possibility alone was enough to keep her motivated.
>
> Sooner than expected, she was promoted to manager and celebrated as the youngest one in the company. She was called a "high flyer" and admired by her peers. Her motivation was through the roof and her energy was buzzing at an all-time high. She was appreciated by her bosses, revered by her colleagues, and admired by her family and friends. What more could she possibly want?
>
> Being the super-achiever that she was, she adapted quickly to her new managerial role without difficulty. In seeing her quick progress, her boss decides to hire a junior to report to her. They needed the extra staff and she was capable of managing someone. She found the challenge daunting and nerve-racking at first, but rose to the occasion, becoming a "boss" for the first time.

When we climb up a ladder, we usually don't focus on the rung we are standing on, but rather the ones to follow. The same applies to the corporate ladder. As we build expertise and experience, growth becomes a priority.

We look to our peers and superiors for inspiration, and our professional achievements can be quite exhilarating. We then cling to our progress and become troubled by plateaus in our careers. Growth, in our minds, becomes a necessary part of our survival.

It's not uncommon for people to form obsessions around growth and career success. By associating our growth with survival, it almost feels necessary, and becomes a compelling driver in our choices and behavior.

Case Study: "Free at Last"

This pattern can be seen in other paths in life. Similar things can be said about careers in academia, sports, and even in one's health. Progress is both addictive and blinding. With our sights set on the rungs above us, and the rewarding nature of growth, the path we are on becomes difficult to veer from. It is only when we struggle or fail that we begin to question the choices we've made, which often comes much later in life.

What does growth mean to you? What areas of your life do you feel a need or drive for growth? Do you associate your growth with survival? Have you had to make any sacrifices in order to grow? If so, what were they and, looking back, were they worth it?

> One day, as she inducts a new member onto her now large and very successful team, she gets asked an interesting question: "Why do we do things this way?" It lands like a slap to the face. "Uh, I don't know…" She stumbles and brushes it aside to continue the meeting. Later that day, as work quiets down, she sits in her office and ponders over that ever so innocent question. It bothers her a great deal, for no reason other than the fact she was ten years into her career with the company now and had no clue how to answer it. *It's just the way we do things*, she thought to herself. But something about that answer didn't sit right with her.
>
> She begins to dig, asking a few of her peers and colleagues. "It's just the way we do things," seemed to be the only answer anybody could offer her. It felt strange that they all had the same thing to say, and eventually she remembered her first boss saying something similar. It was almost like a mantra they all knew but didn't question.

> Their methods were complex and rooted in corporate history, their choices handed down from generation to generation, and she had accepted the baton without question. As her exploration continued, she began to understand why their methods were so poorly understood by the majority of her colleagues—they were rife with regulatory concerns and restrictions, were difficult to explain, and even questionable at times. She was venturing down the rabbit hole, and the more she dug, the more she regretted it.
>
> They had used chemicals in certain products, something she already knew but never really understood. They adhered to regulatory requirements but something about that didn't feel responsible enough to her. Some of the chemicals they used were known carcinogens, and while they were well within legal limits, their use didn't seem to outweigh the risks. Nowhere on their labels did they warn their consumers of this—something her colleague in Regulatory Affairs said "wasn't legally required" and "would only scare them." These words echoed in her head for days to come, but what haunted her was the fact that she was only just beginning to understand how the monstrous machine she worked for really operated.

When we are very young, "That's just the way it's done!" is a perfectly acceptable explanation as to why we do something a certain way. We're expected to follow the instructions and guidance of our parents and teachers without question. We're learning the basics of life, after all, and don't necessarily need to know why things are done in a certain way. They know better and our trust in them supersedes our curiosity. But as we mature, we begin to understand the idea of causation and realize that outcomes can be influenced by the choices we make. Eventually, knowledge becomes a necessity for us and a lack of it prevents us from being able to take full responsibility.

A lack of knowledge also allows us to play the victim. Not understanding how something works or why it is done becomes a justification for not taking responsibility. We do this with our food choices, material purchases and, very often, in our careers. We frequently mimic our childhood behavior—blindly trusting our leaders, bosses, and those we hold in reverence because "they know better," alleviating ourselves from the responsibility of the choices we make. Once again, this stems from our survival instinct and allows us to move past any pain or anguish. But in doing so, we remove a powerful motivator for real change: guilt. This emotion contributes to the survival of others, by signaling a problem with a choice that we have made. By numbing ourselves in this way, we stifle any motivation to seek a better path and maintain focus on the one we're on.

Can you recall any choices you made in life where you didn't fully understand why things were done in a certain way? What do you feel you could have or should have understood better?

> The feeling of pride that once filled Amy's chest was now replaced with something more sinister. It felt heavy and dark—a mix of shame and frustration—and it weighed her down. The work she did no longer felt empowering and exciting. Every decision made her doubt herself. She was suddenly aware of every little detail and felt a sense of responsibility she hadn't until now. She realized more clearly than ever how tangibly she was affecting the lives of her

> consumers. Looking back over the years, it seemed as if only the positive impact of her work had was celebrated. The customer complaints and "conspiracy theorists" haunting the company's social media channels were often laughed at, shrugged off or offered canned responses. They were the minority, declared a nuisance, and never given much spotlight. From the training material she received when she was first hired, to the promotions and raises she received over the years, to the bureaucratic procedures in place to protect corporate secrets—there were so many layers that kept her biased toward the interests of the company. And, with those biases in place, it was easy to only ever see and feel the good in what she did. She was a drone and finally realized it. As her world came crumbling down around her, the reality of the role she played in influencing people's decisions and the influence she had on the lives of her consumers was clearer than ever. She was blind to the mistakes she had made. But now, for the first time, she was wide awake.

Waking up to any truth can inundate us with an amalgam of emotions. Realizing our role in something damaging can be quite challenging to accept. It is natural to feel some level of guilt and shame, both of which are quite powerful and difficult to process. If tackled in a healthy manner, these emotions can become fuel for positive change. However, we tend to want to avoid or numb them—yet another product of our innate desire to survive and flourish.

Guilt and shame are quite often associated with how others may perceive us. Our desire to avoid these feelings, while wanting to fit in and be accepted, can drive us to avoid or hide from a truth that needs to be addressed. Though, with some self-compassion, courage and an open mind, we can take the first step in making substantial and tangible change in spite of these feelings—opening our eyes and accepting things for what they truly are.

Have you faced a time in your professional or personal life where you realized you were inadvertently contributing to something negative or damaging? What did you feel when you came to this realization? How did you process those feelings? How did making this realization change the way you work, live, or think?

> Her first reaction was to find someone to blame: her bosses for training her and, ultimately, brainwashing her; the company's leadership for setting the goals that led to all of this happening in the first place; the board, for overseeing everything but not saying anything; the shareholders for inadvertently creating the pressure that resulted in everyone being more focused on commercial goals; the government, for not having been stringent enough with their regulations. She saw herself a victim in all of this and finding a perpetrator was imperative.
> As she went through the long list of people who trained, guided and supported her over the years—the supervisors, managers and directors who took her under their wings—she felt betrayed. "How could they be okay with all of this?" she thought to herself. "They're good people." The idea that they were all aware and simply okay with the recklessness of the organization didn't seem realistic. They were good people. Just as she was.
>
> She was a driving force behind the organization, never intending to do any harm but ended up realizing her part in it. They were all likely caught up in the same whirlwind as she was, and, therefore, no single person or group was to blame. If

> this was the case, then the problem was the system itself, within which they all operated.
>
> Her years of education set her up for a corporate career. Her family and friends pushed her to succeed and kept her passion and drive for growth alive over the years. Her material desires and financial interests kept her sights set on the next promotion, raise, or bonus. Her colleagues and peers and the competitive nature of the business world kept all of them distracted, racing against the clock in a fight for survival. It was a multifaceted issue and she realized that her mentality and choices, as well as everyone else's, were to blame. They were all speeding through life, making quick decisions, rapidly innovating to remain competitive, and following loosely defined legal and moral guidelines, because that's all they really had the time and resources to do.

Playing the blame game is very easy. Simply point the finger and move it around until you find something or someone to be at fault. But, when it comes to systemic issues, you may find yourself struggling to do so.

We live within a complex system of systems, all of which contribute to each other in some way or another. Within each of these systems resides an intricate, co-dependent ecosystem that makes finding a single source to a problem virtually impossible.

The truth, that many people fail to recognize or even acknowledge, is that every player within a system is to blame for its outcomes. All of us play a role and contribute to the collective outcome of the systems we are part of—just as each individual snowflake contributes to the formation of a snowy hill. Just as our actions may contribute to a negative outcome, we can shift our thinking, alter our choices and create a more positive future together.

Can you identify the role you play within a wider system? Over what areas of your life do you have the greatest and most obvious influence? In which ones do you feel you have the least?

> As she reflected on her career, she realized how mindless much of her behavior was over the years. She had been so focused on the challenges and objectives that came her way that she had blocked out everything else. She didn't have the time or the energy to do more than what was needed to get the job done. She rushed through meals, sped to and from meetings, and worked through nights and weekends—frequently neglecting her own mental, emotional, and physical needs for the sake of her work. Being so distracted, it was no wonder she found herself facing so many unanswered questions so far into her career.

One of our most deluded beliefs is that time is abundant. While we may often complain about not having enough time to do the things we want or frequently indulge in pseudo-philosophical statements like "life is short," we tend to behave as if we have all the time in the world. We procrastinate and tend to put things off assuming we will have the time to get around to it at some point. Before we know it, days turn into weeks, and weeks turn into months and years. Eventually, we reach a point where we look back on our choices and wish we had been more careful with the time we were given.

Our focus tends to be on the tasks and opportunities that are most urgent, lucrative, or satisfying. We often prioritize our actions based on gratification rather than essentiality, and these choices contribute to the development of a mindless habit that shifts our focus to short-term outcomes, rather than future implications.

Looking back over your life, how mindful do you feel you have been? Have you taken the time to appreciate the finer things? Do you have a list of things you would like to do, but never seem to get around to them? In what ways can you become more mindful in your work and life?

> Amy pinpointed times in her life where she could have benefited most from some critical life advice. Her teachers in high-school could have taught her to weigh out the pros and cons of a decision. Her parents and relatives could have been better examples of how to balance out career, health, and life early on. Her managers and mentors in her junior years could have laid out processes and procedures to better comprehend corporate decisions. Early influence seemed to be the key, so she decided to focus on setting up the next generation for success. This meant relieving herself from the need to see immediate results, but at least she would become more mindful in her own work as she tried to positively influence those around her.

It's not always the obvious contributions that have the greatest influence on our lives. Every interaction and experience shift our trajectory, but sometimes only slightly and therefore easily overlooked. Small lessons in childhood, for example, can extrapolate into larger ones later in life. A series of seemingly unrelated experiences can come together to alter our behavior and thinking patterns. With time, the bigger picture becomes more obvious to us, but if we can learn to recognize and appreciate the contributions to our lives, perhaps we can become more mindful of our own.

Has there been a time in your life where you've learned a lesson through a surprising or unrelated experience? What have been your greatest influences in life? Do you recognize the impact particular people had early on in your life or career?

> She returned to work with renewed energy and began asking questions similar to what she was once asked, those that kick-started the journey she was now on. She began questioning why things were done in certain ways, and what could be done better. She applied a curiosity that was reminiscent of her childhood. She saw the world in a new, wondrous light, and felt an excitement she hadn't felt in years.
>
> Over the next several weeks, she noticed that it didn't take much to apply her new principles to the way that she worked. Being mindless in her work was a lot more complicated than being mindful. She began by identifying a purpose, or at least understanding existing ones, behind each big decision to be made. She would do her own due diligence so that she wouldn't find herself not knowing why something was done in a particular way or what its impact was. She would learn, debate, challenge, and finally, make a conscious and deliberate choice. No longer would she blindly sign things off because "that's the way it's done." Never again would she make a decision in haste to simply meet her targets. She owed her consumers her time, effort, and care and accepted her

> responsibility toward them. Her days of mindlessness were over.

Unlearning unhealthy behavior is just as difficult as learning a new one. Both require genuine effort and a real commitment to change. But once we are ready to take a new path in life, we can revive a few childhood qualities that may help us along the way. We can replace the fear of taking the path less trodden with curiosity and an adventurous spirit. Both of these qualities are abundant within us but suppressed by our frequently triggered survival instincts and the busy nature of maturity. If we can find the courage to rebel against the norm (and ourselves) in favor of a better future for our children and theirs to follow, we will come to realize that we are not alone… but leading the way.

What parts of this story resonated with you? Do you see opportunities in your own life to change the way you think, feel, or act? What legacy do you want to leave your children or future generations? What are the next steps you may want to take in your own life toward a more mindful future?

7. The Next Step

As children, we naturally seek out human connection. We love indiscriminately, unconditionally and with genuine emotion. But somewhere along the way, we lose this innate connection to the world and begin to forget what it means to truly love another human, wanting nothing in return but to be loved back.

In the Arabic language, the word for "human" can be derived from a root word that means "forgetful," the reasoning being that humans are quick to forget. Take our birth into this world as an example. It's a process that one could only assume is quite traumatic, yet despite it being our first (and possibly quite shocking) experience, we remember nothing of it. Our forgetfulness is necessary for our survival. It allows us to make the mental and emotional room we need to process more important matters in life, but it's a tool that is easy to overuse and abuse.

The internet and technology have made it easier for us to disconnect from one another. The suffering of the world can seem very movie-like, almost unreal at times. It's harder to feel empathetic toward something or someone that's so far removed from you.

It's even harder to worry about the generations to come, being as far downstream from us as they are.

In the business world, we tend to dehumanize the people we have influence or power over. We label them "customers" or "consumers." We even refer to our own people as "employees" or "resources." We refer to people in the collective and it's harder to feel empathy toward a large group, even harder when we forget that we're talking about human beings.

Accept it or not, you are influential, and your influence reaches far beyond your own existence and surroundings. We all are. In our fight for survival in this world, dispersed across the globe and consequently disconnected from one another, we've lost this realization. But in realizing this, we can begin to accept responsibility, which is essential if we're going to change the course of history.

Whether you're a parent, a teacher, an employee of a large multinational organization, a government official, or just a student, you have an influence over the people around you. In fact, you can influence all living things around you. Every choice has a consequence. Every choice. Every piece of trash you throw out. Every light switch you turn on. Every human interaction. Every business decision. Some have greater consequences than others but they all do nonetheless.

You are an important part of humanity. You are valuable and significant. Our planet may be nothing more than a speck of dust in the vast universe within which it resides, but to say that it's insignificant would be ignorant. After all, small as it may be in the cosmos, it's the only planet (so far) with any life on it. It may be small, but it is unique and special; worthy of marvel and respect. The same goes for you, and every human being.

You are as unique, special and worthy of marvel and respect as this planet. But this honor doesn't come without a price. We owe it to this beautiful planet, and all of its inhabitants—those that are already here and those to come—to honor and protect what we've been given.

We were all once able to love others in the purest sense of the word. We cried when others cried. We laughed when others laughed. We were once connected but have long since forgotten. Let us try to remember and to reconnect. And perhaps we can begin to create a world that is ruled by the most beautiful aspects of our humanity.

You don't have to want to change the entire world, but the truth is that you will in some way. We all will. We're interconnected and every choice we make lays a stone in the path ahead of us. Our children and grandchildren and theirs after them will live in the world we build for them. We don't need to create the next big thing or become the next big anyone to make a positive and constructive contribution. All we have to do is try.

Every effort, every decision, no matter how small, does and will make a difference. We may have little or no control over the outcomes of our efforts, but we have full control over our intentions and desires to do good. If we lead with love, its effects will ripple through the ages. Never underestimate the power of a single choice.